To the Houck family,
May you always have
great adventures!

Becky

BLAZING A TRAIL

The Story of Minna Anthony Common

Written by
Becky Ferrigno

Illustrated by
Jennifer M. Varn

Pocket Jennifer Publishing • New York

Pocket Jennifer Publishing

Pocket Jennifer Publishing
Beacon, NY 12508
www.pocketjenniferpublishing.com

Cover and Interior Design: Jennifer M. Varn
Editor: Molly Farrell
Interior text set at: Times; Cover text set at: Papyrus

Artwork created by a mixed media of acrylic, pastel, and matte glue
www.jmvillustrations.com

Library of Congress Catalog Number: 2019907805
ISBN: 978-0-9967173-4-2
1. Picture Book - Non Fiction 2. Conservation 3. Nature 4. Biography

First Printing, 2019

Printed in the United States of America

Dedications:

To Vera and Molly whose rocking chair meetings made this book possible.

- Becky

To my mother, sisters, nieces, and partner who inspire me daily to keep persisting.

- Jennifer

Have you ever had a time in your life
where something awful has happened?

Have you faced a problem so hard that you are not sure how you will move past it?

Well, if you have ever been through something like this, you have faced adversity.

For some people, adversity defines their lives and prevents them from growing.

For others, like Minna Anthony Common, adversity provides the springboard to a lifetime of triumphs.

On September 11, 1882, Minna Capron Anthony was born into an ordinary upstate New York family.

She had a mother, a father, and an 8-year old sister named Hattie.

If life had continued on that path, she could have had a very ordinary upbringing and lived a very ordinary life.

Sadly when Minna was only a few months old her mother, Margaret, contracted diphtheria.

Her death changed the course of her daughter's life forever.

During the chaos following Margaret's death, Minna's uncle took his 2-month-old niece to live with her grandmother.

Minna was raised by her grandmother, Amelia Brown Anthony, in Watertown, NY.

When Minna was eight years old, Amelia built one of the first cottages at Thousand Island Park on Wellesley Island in the St. Lawrence River.

While it was being built, Amelia and Minna lived in a tent on the site. Once built, they spent every summer there.

It was from these visits that Minna's love of nature developed.

Minna was an excellent student and graduated with honors from Watertown High School in 1899.

She was offered a full-tuition scholarship to St. Lawrence University but her grandmother disapproved of women going to college and would not let her go.

Once again, Minna was faced with adversity. Did she give up on her dream? No, she did not. Instead, she took a different path to reach her goal.

Minna completed a one-year postgraduate
course at Watertown High School that
prepared her to teach public school.

Her first teaching position was in the
Brownville-Glen Park School District.

When the weather was bad, Minna would take the trolley to work, but on nice days, she would ride her bike the five miles from Watertown to Brownville.

For four years she taught first grade and tutored children.

In her free time, she studied botany (the study of plants) with a friend who majored in the subject at college and took painting and sketching lessons from a high school art teacher in Watertown.

During the summer months, she stayed at her grandmother's cottage in Thousand Island Park and took courses through the Cornell University Extension Services.

One of her teachers was Anna Botsford Comstock, who is widely recognized as the mother of nature education.

In 1904 she married James Allison Common and together they had six children. Minna's family expected her to not have a life outside of the home after marriage.

Minna refused to let this role change stop her from doing what she loved. Instead, she taught her children to love nature.

With her curly hair wound up in a bun, wearing a long skirt and a basket on her arm containing a hammer, ink, pen, and cardboard to sketch on, Minna took her daughters and son on countless hikes through the woods.

It was on one of those hikes that she noticed that the trees behind her cottage had splashes of paint on them.

She went down to the Thousand Island Park Association with a fire in her eyes and demanded to know what was going on.

The association told her that the trees were going to be cut down for lumber. Minna convinced them to lumber elsewhere by suggesting that those woods would be an excellent place for a nature trail.

In August of 1935, the Rock Ridges Nature Trail opened.

Minna and her children maintained the mile and a half long trail from that day until her death.

Eventually, Minna even began writing about nature for newspapers and magazines!

From 1922 to her death in 1950, she published articles in the *New York Times*, the *Christian Science Monitor,* and the *Watertown Daily Times*.

Her way of looking at and learning about nature was so radically different than what people were thinking at the time that many New Yorkers took notice!

In 1950, Minna Anthony Common died from a heart attack. However, her children made sure that her work and her name would never be forgotten.

In the late 1960's her daughter, Catherine Common Johnson, organized the sale of private land to New York State.

She then contacted Albany, the state capital, and secured the funds required to build a nature center in the woods her mother loved so well.

Since 1969, The Minna Anthony Common Nature
Center has been a place where families can come
to enjoy and learn about the beautiful nature that
Minna Anthony Common fell in love with and
worked to preserve so many years ago.

For women like Minna, adversity prepares
you to be strong and determined when you
believe there is something worth fighting for.

Author's Note

Minna Anthony Common's ancestors were among the first settlers in the Watertown area in the early 1800's. After her mother's death, Minna's father took Hattie and moved to Minnesota where he eventually remarried and raised a second family. He never returned for his second daughter.

Minna's Grandmother, Amelia Brown Common

Minna's sister, Hattie

In the early 1940's, Hattie would return to visit her sister. During that visit, she taught Minna how to use oil paint, and from that point on, Minna only painted with oil. The sisters never saw each other again.

Minna was a prolific writer. From 1922 on, she contributed two articles weekly to the *Watertown Daily Times*- one on birds and one on flowers. This was in addition to her contributions to the *New York Times, Herald Tribune, Christian Science Monitor, Bird Lore* and the *Audubon Society*.

From 1926 until her death, Minna served as the Official Federal Bird Observer for the Jefferson County area and kept the National Fish and Wildlife Service informed of bird migration. She conducted a yearly local bird census for the Audubon Society and ran the North Country Bird Club, which she had founded. Four days prior to her death, she spoke at a meeting of the Watertown Superintendent and Principals on the necessity of a course on nature study in the school system.

After Minna's death, her daughter, Catherine Johnson, used her position on the Thousand Island Park Commission to help New York State acquire privately held land on Wellesley Island for a state-run park. She then lobbied Albany for the money required to build the Minna Anthony Common Nature Center.

Like her mother, Catherine Johnson "knew how to get things done."

Sources:

Coe, M. (n.d.). Minna Anthony Common and Catherine Common Johnson: Two Uncommon Women: Mother and Daughter, Naturalists and Artists. Retrieved August 5, 2017, from https://auuwjeffco.wordpress.com/women-in-history/minna-anthony-common-catherine-common-johnson

Emerson, E. C. (Ed.). (1898). History of Brownville, NY From Our County and It's People. A Descriptive Work on Jefferson County, NY. Boston History Company. Retrieved August 5, 2017, from history.rays-place.com/ny/brownville-ny.htm.

Fulmer, Z & Taylor, N. (1994) Rock Ridges Nature Trail

Glen Park. (n.d.). Retrieved August 5, 2017, from https://jeffco.wikispaces.com/Glen+Park

Kane, A. (Director). (2016, November 3). Vera Uncut: Interview of Vera Common Parmiter by Molly, L. Farrell, Minna Anthony Common Nature Center Director [Video file]. Retrieved June 29, 2017, from https://vimeo.com/190033768

Karamessimes, J. C. (1976, May). Information for a Biography of My Mother, Minna Anthony Common for my sister Catherine Common Johnson [Scholarly project].

Parmiter, V. (2017) Rock Ridges Nature Trails Recollections

Acknowledgements:

Molly, the conduit for all things Minna, including photos, biographies and an amazing two-hour long video. It is your knowledge and passion that started this project.
Vera Common Parmiter and her daughter Claudia for sharing their family photos, stories and time. I truly appreciate your insight and willingness to share Minna with me.

Vera, Anneke, David and Molly for editing the book, discussing commas and providing excellent editorial help.

Dad for all of the free legal advice and Andy for filming the amazing interview with Vera that introduced me to Minna.

Brian, and the rest of my family who supported this project from the beginning and gave me the time and the space to write.

About the Author:

Becky Ferrigno is an author on a mission to write about children and adults who overcome adversity and live incredible lives. **Blazing A Trail: The Story of Minna Anthony Common** is her debut children's book.

Her work on sensory processing disorder, parenting and loss have been featured on The Mighty, Motherly, Today's Parent and Modern Loss. Becky's first book series, which is in development, focuses on introducing children and adults to Sensory Processing Disorder. She is also the author of **Across the Water: Teaching Irish Music At Home and Abroad** (R&L Education, 2010). Becky has a Bachelor and Masters Degree in Music Education and has been a public school educator for the last 13 years.

About the Illustrator:

Jennifer M. Varn is a singer songwriter and an illustrator. Her focus is to communicate emotional messages through images. Her debut picture book, **My Day... A Long Distance Lullaby** combines multimedia illustration with songwriting. Ms. Varn is a folk musician in style but also in ethos. Her music follows the folk tradition of social activism through song and seeks to bridge the gap between adult and youth understandings of complex and difficult emotions. She also seeks to bridge the gaps between different and disparate communities in her work by creating emotionally rich stories that resonate across multiple boundaries. To view more of her work, please visit her online studio, JMV Illustrations: www.jmvillustrations.com

Get Outside Like Minna!

The following pages are for you to draw and write down your very

own observations and experiences with nature!

For fun outdoor activity ideas, follow author, Becky Ferrigno's blog:
www.beckyferrigno.com/blog

_____

_____

_____

_____

_____

CPSIA information can be obtained
at www.ICGtesting.com
Printed in the USA
BVHW060542231019
561821BV00003B/5/P